Incredible
Sea Creatures

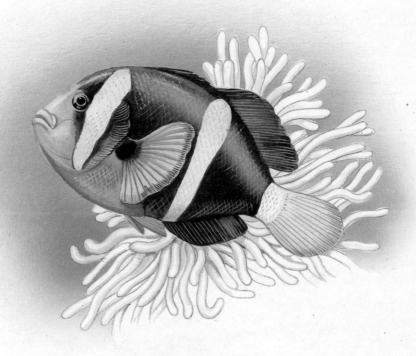

LEVEL  READER

READING LEVEL
2
GRADES 1 TO 3

Written by Kathryn Knight
Illustrated by Edizioni Larus S.p.A.

Copyright © 2014 Bendon Publishing International, Inc.
All rights reserved. Printed in Haining, Zhejiang, China.

Coral Reef

Coral reefs are beautiful underwater areas where incredible sea creatures live. Many different kinds of coral create the reef—some shaped like a tree, others like a flower, and some like a brain!

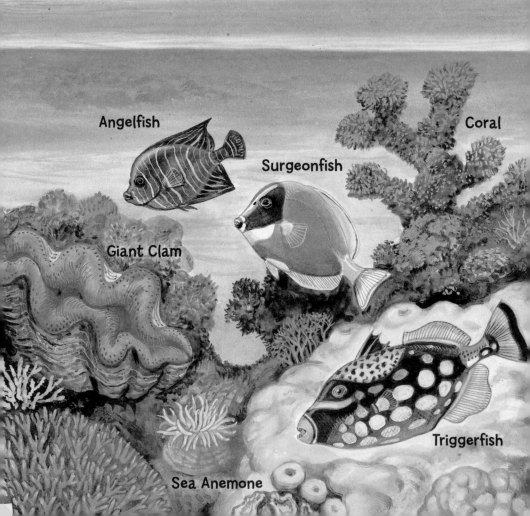

Angelfish

Surgeonfish

Coral

Giant Clam

Triggerfish

Sea Anemone

Inside their hard outer skeletons live tiny jellylike coral animals, called *polyps* (**paul**-ips), that build this amazing undersea world.

Parrotfish

Dusky Grouper

Clownfish

Yellow Boxfish

Golden Butterflyfish

Many of the coral reef creatures are slow-moving and may never leave the reef. Some flutter through the water, like the mini-finned seahorse. Others slide along the seabed floor, like the many-armed starfish. Even the sea urchin, an animal that looks like a plant, is able to creep slowly over rocks and sand.

Seahorse

Sea Urchin

Starfish

Sea Anemone

Some of the loveliest reef creatures are the sea *anemones* (uh-**nem**-uh-neez). Some are small, no bigger than a grape. Others can be 6 feet wide. Beware—those pretty petal-like tentacles contain a poison that stuns small fish and other prey.

Sea Sponge

Sponges come in all sorts of unusual shapes. Their skeletons are made of *spongin* (**spuhn**-jin), a stretchy material. This is where we get the natural sponges we use to wash with.

Beadlet Anemone

Sea Anemone

Sea Sponge

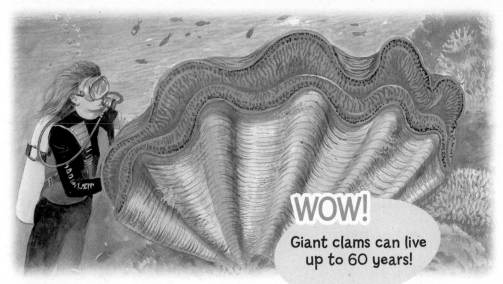

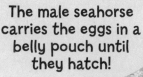

WOW!
Giant clams can live up to 60 years!

Giant Clam

The giant clam can grow to 5 feet across and weigh 500 pounds. It opens its huge shell to feed on plankton and *algae* (**al**-jee), tiny animal and plantlike life forms.

Seahorse

FUN FACT!
The male seahorse carries the eggs in a belly pouch until they hatch!

The seahorse has a strange shape for a fish. Its tail can wind around water plants to hold it in place. To move, the little seahorse beats its fanlike fin.

Sea Slug

Sea slugs are called the jewels of the sea. They range from 4 to 20 inches long. See the feathery fringe on its back? That helps the sea slug take in oxygen from the water.

WOW!
Sea slugs are pretty—but poisonous!

Starfish

A starfish uses its many arms to move about and catch food. It wraps its arms around a clam and pulls the shell apart to get at the soft animal inside.

WOW!
A starfish can re-grow an entire body—from one arm!

Jellyfish

Jellyfish (or jellies) are not fish. They are soft sea creatures that float in open water. Their long tentacles deliver a painful, poisonous sting that kills its prey.

WOW!

Some jellies are 6 feet wide!

Coral

Coral may look like a plant, but it is an animal. This hard outer part protects the soft polyps inside. Each polyp sends out tiny stinging tentacles to catch plankton.

Corals are related to jellies!

FUN FACT!

Spotted Moray Eel

What's that snake-like creature peeking out from between the rocks? It's a fish—called a moray eel. Never wave your hand in front of a moray eel. It might mistake it for an octopus and bite it!

WOW!
Moray eels can reach 6 feet long!

Ribbon Eel

Male ribbon eels are electric-blue. The females are completely yellow. The tube-like nostrils that flare at the tips give the ribbon eel an excellent sense of smell.

WOW!
Ribbon eels are all males at birth. Some later become female and turn yellow!

Sharks

The largest predators in the reef are the sharks. Just like many of the other reef creatures, sharks have no bones. They only have firm tissue called *cartilage* (**car**-tuh-lij), like the cartilage that forms your ears.

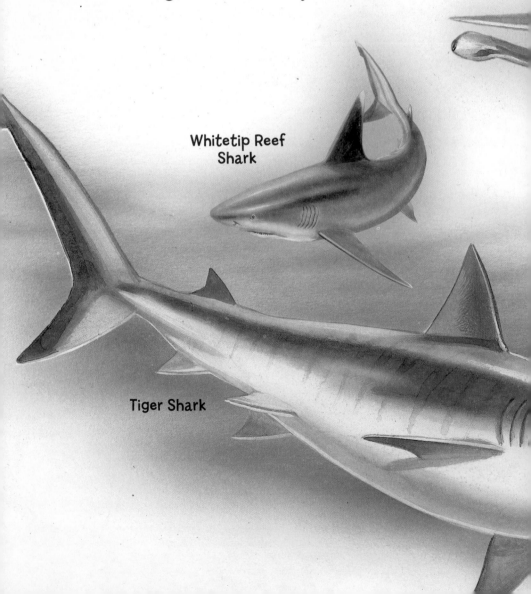

Whitetip Reef Shark

Tiger Shark

Hammerhead Shark

The hammerhead shark has a head that looks like a hammer. Each end has an eye and a nostril. This shape helps the shark see and smell and move well through the water.

Stingray

Stingrays are related to sharks. Like sharks, they have no bones. They are flat fish with wide fins. They flap their fins to move through the water.

The stingray has a sharp barb on the end of its tail. It has poison in this barb. When the stingray strikes with its tail, it stings!

WOW!
Stingrays can grow to
6½ feet long!

Clownfish

This tiny fish was named for having stripes like a clown's face. Clownfish are able to live with sea anemones because they are not affected by their poisonous tentacles.

FUN FACT!
The clownfish takes care of its sea anemone "home" by grooming it!

Clown Triggerfish

The *dorsal* (**door**-suhl) fin on the back of the clown triggerfish can be "locked" to stay straight up. This allows the fish to be tightly wedged between branches of coral.

WOW!
The clown triggerfish can bite through metal!

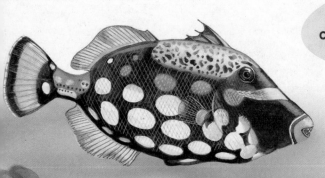

Stoplight Parrotfish

Stoplight Parrotfish crunch into the hard outer skeleton of coral with their parrot-like jaw. Then they digest the soft polyps. What happens to the crunched-up skeleton part? It comes out as fine, white sand!

WOW!

The stoplight parrotfish changes color as it ages. Some are red, some green, some yellow!

Miniata Grouper

Groupers are powerful predators with large mouths. The miniata grouper's bright color and spots help it hide among the coral.

WOW!
Groupers suck in prey with one big-mouth gulp!

Palette Surgeonfish

This fish (also called a blue tang) has spines at the base of its tail that are razor-sharp—like a surgeon's knives. Fishermen must be very careful when pulling in nets that may hold one of these fish.

FUN FACT!
Surgeonfish eat algae with teeth that are bristly like a toothbrush!

Trumpetfish

What an odd and incredible fish! Its "trumpet"
snout has a hooked beak that easily traps tiny
fish that it sucks in.

Lionfish

The lionfish's elegant fins sweep through
the water like butterfly wings. But, beware!
The spines in its fins inject poison.

Porcupinefish

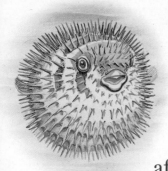

The porcupinefish is also called a blowfish. It is able to make itself larger (and rounder) by gulping water. If a predator keeps after it, its spiny scales will pop up—like a porcupine's quills! Ouch!

FUN FACT!
A porcupinefish has huge eyes to help it look for food at night!

Stonefish

The stonefish is one of the most dangerous animals in the sea. It hardly moves on the rocky seabed, and algae grows all over its bumpy skin. Fish swim up close to what looks like a stone—and are soon made into a meal.

WOW!
The stonefish has a spine on its back that injects a deadly poison if you step on it!

Humphead Wrasse

This fish is a whopper! Up to 6 feet long and 300 pounds! Its head has stripes and swirls that form interesting patterns. Native people of New Zealand used to tattoo themselves with designs from the humphead wrasse.

WOW!
This curious fish will swim close to divers and let them pet it!

WOW!
A mother sea turtle comes ashore to lay about 150 eggs in a hole in the sand!

Hawksbill Sea Turtle

This graceful sea turtle is 2 to 3 feet long. Its shell has beautiful yellow and black markings. Look at its sharp, curved mouth—it's just like a hawk's bill. These turtles use their flippers like wings, gliding smoothly through the water.

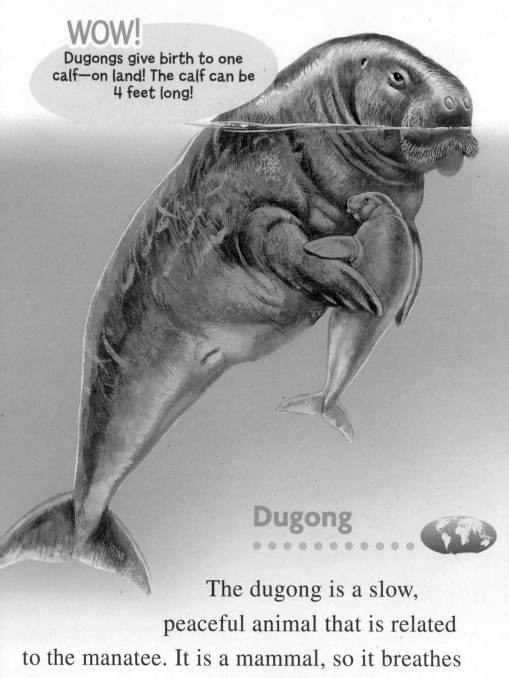

WOW!
Dugongs give birth to one calf—on land! The calf can be 4 feet long!

Dugong

• • • • • • • • • • • •

The dugong is a slow, peaceful animal that is related to the manatee. It is a mammal, so it breathes air at the water's surface. It does not have much hair, but it has thick whiskers. It feeds on sea grasses and water plants, usually during the day.

Ocean Sunfish

Out in the ocean, far from the reef, is the largest bony fish in the world—the ocean sunfish. It is 5 to 10 feet long and can weigh up to 5,000 pounds. It starts out as a tiny *fry* (baby fish) with a normal tail fin. This fin stops growing, but the rest of its body grows to a huge size.

FUN FACT!
Sunfish sometimes float sideways on the ocean surface and "sunbathe"!

Blenny

The little blenny is found along the coasts of tropical and cold seas. Its long body makes it look like an eel. It has two whiskerlike growths on its head called *cirri* (**seer**-eye) and eyes at the top of its head.

WOW!
Blennies have slimy skin and no scales!

Black Goby

The black goby lives in waters around Europe. Do you see its large front fins that touch the seafloor? It uses those to hold itself to a rock while resting or waiting for prey to come along.

FUN FACT!
Male black gobies guard their eggs against younger male gobies called "sneakers."

Common Octopus

The octopus is an intelligent animal with eight long arms. Each arm is lined with two rows of suckers. The octopus is an excellent hunter. Once it spots its prey, it slides close to it, then leaps and traps it with its arms. Its mouth has a bony beak that can break into even the hardest shells.

WOW!

An octopus can squirt a cloud of dark ink at a predator—and then scoot away into the sea!

Anglerfish

Some sea creatures live in the dark depths of the ocean—such as the anglerfish. This fearsome-looking fish has a huge mouth with a double row of sharp teeth. Its rough skin helps it blend in with the sea floor.

The anglerfish has a "fishing pole" that grows out of its head. It wiggles it to attract a fish. The anglerfish strikes and (gulp!) swallows the fish.

WOW!

There are thousands more incredible creatures that live beneath the waves!